This Book Of Joy Belongs To

RARE!

Color Test Page

MOTOCROSS

SPORT CHALLENGE

Never Stop dreaming

NEVER

Give up

ON YOUR

DREAMS

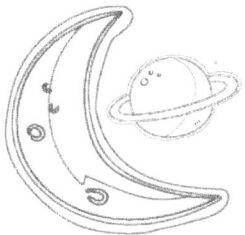

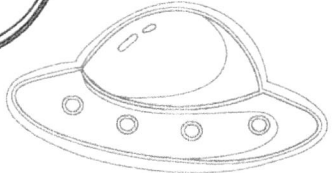

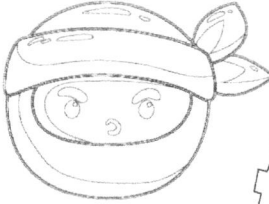

be fearless

WHY BE NORMAL?

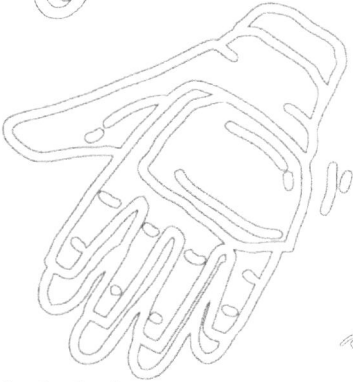

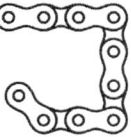

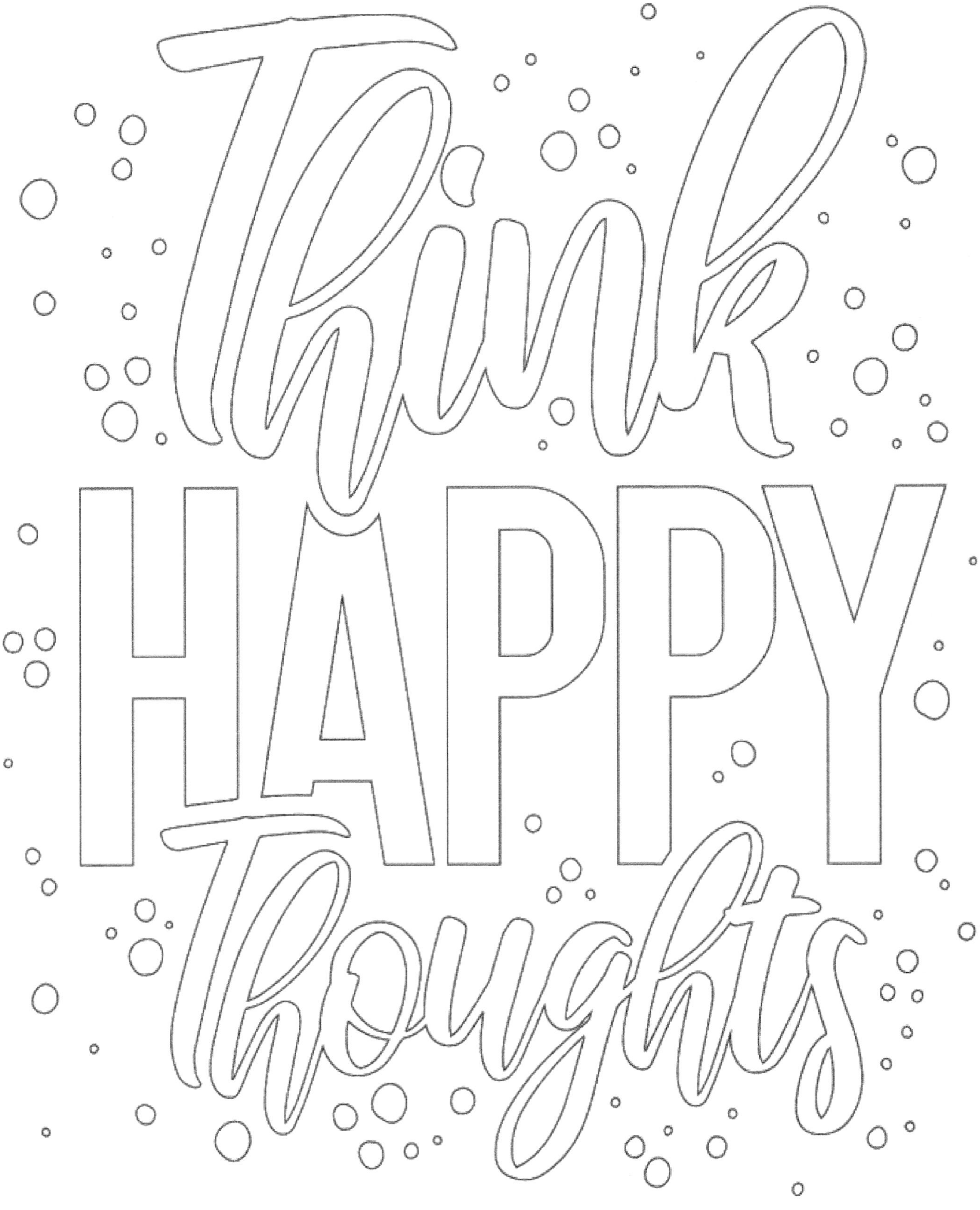
Think
HAPPY
Thoughts

Stay Humble

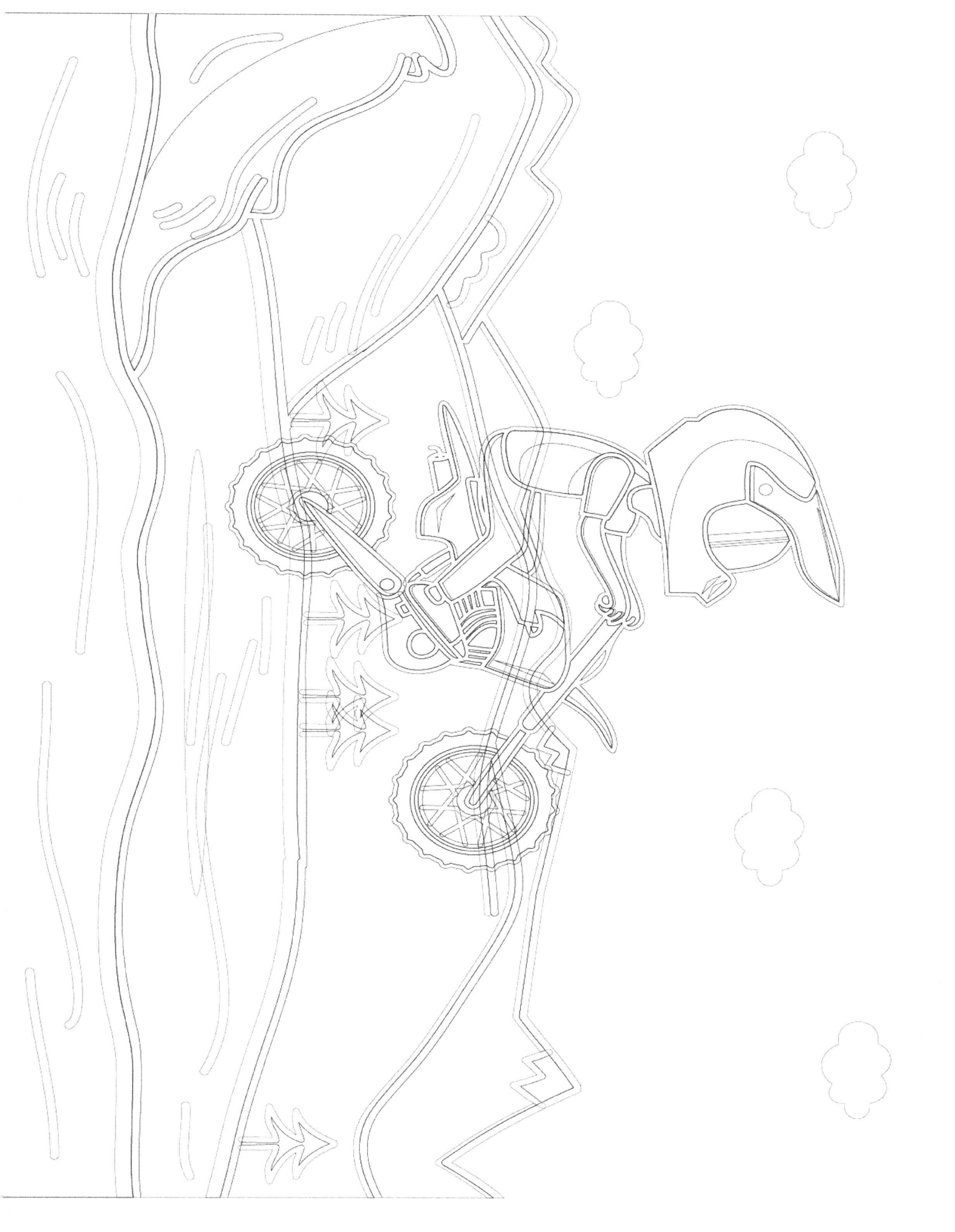

BE Strong AND Courageous

You Light Up my life

THIS LLAMA DOESN'T WANT YOUR DRAMA

Today will be a Good Day

Do what Brings you Joy

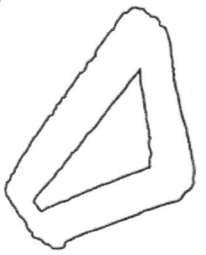

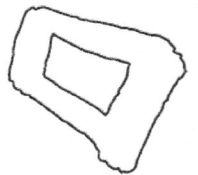

LOVE
HATE
LOVE

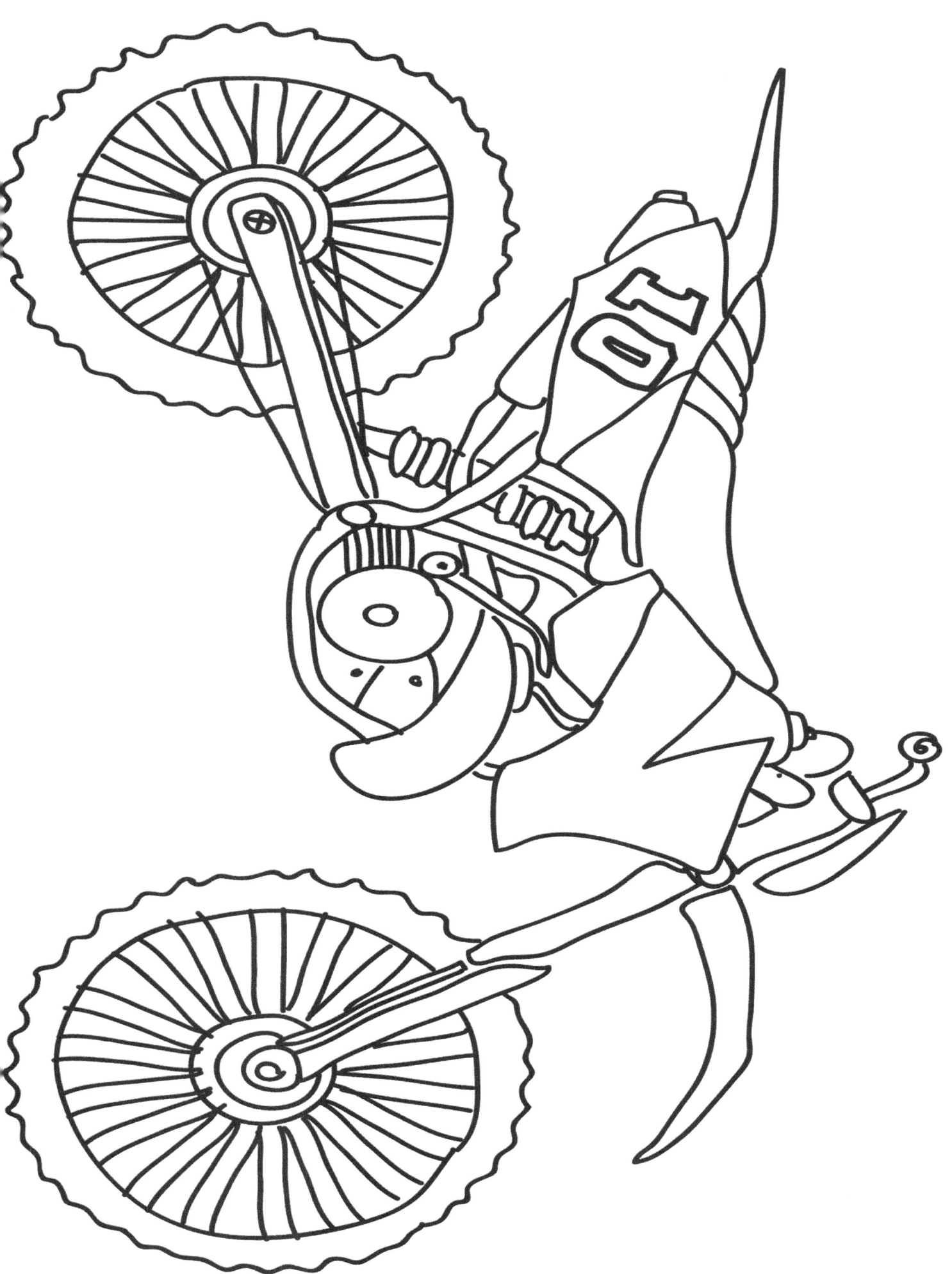

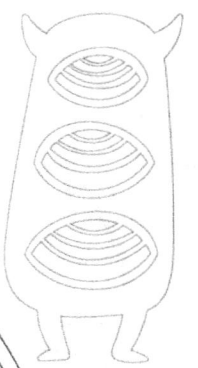

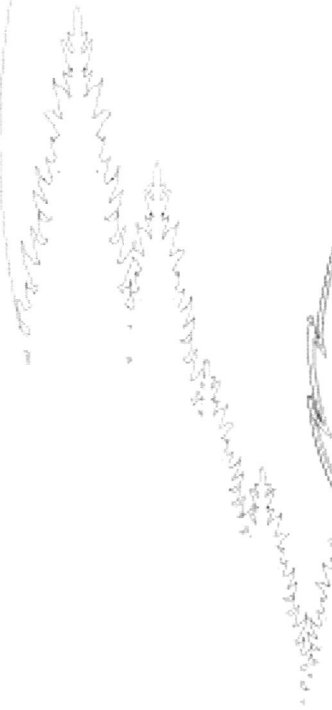

BE BRAVE WITH YOUR Life

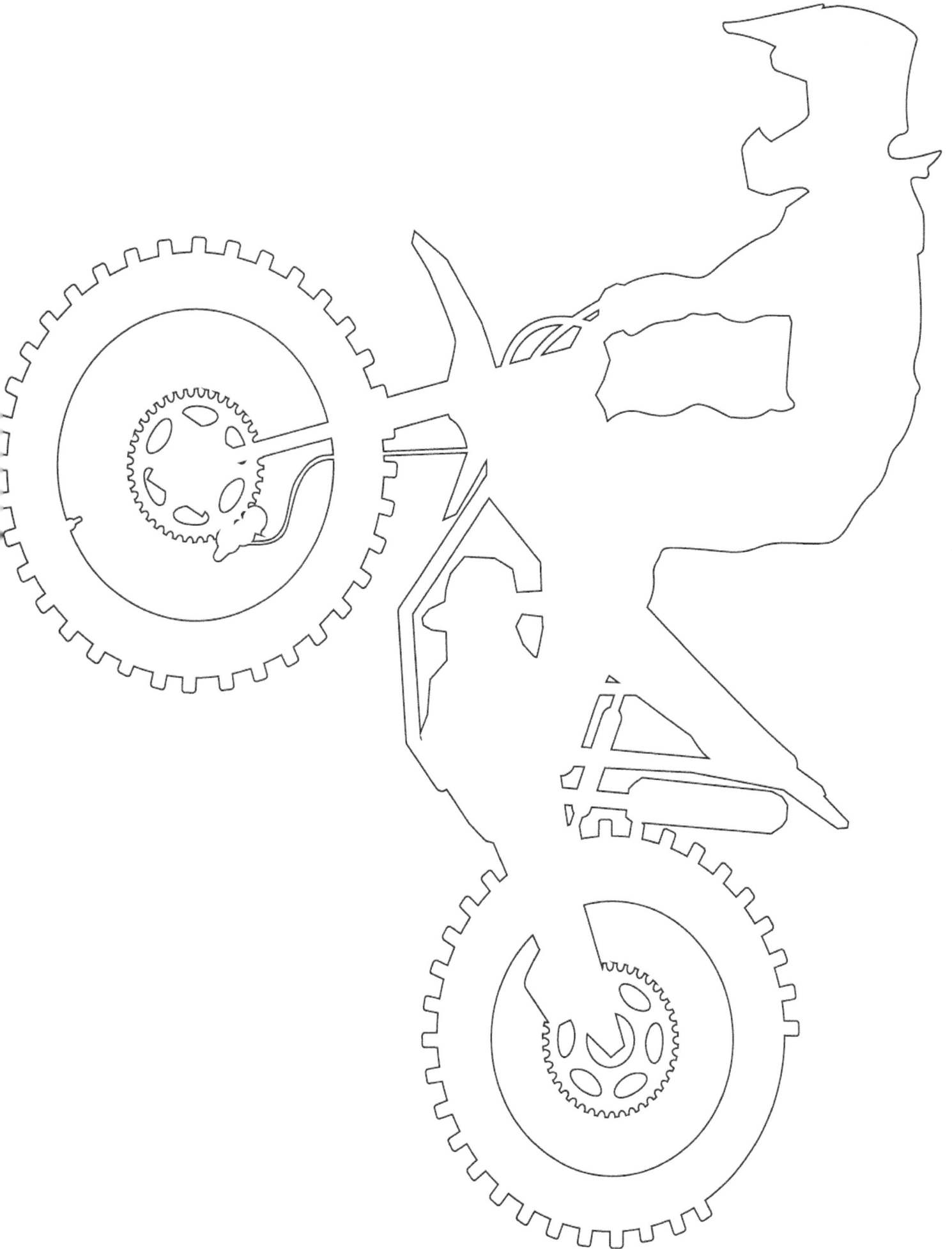

Pray More

Worry Less

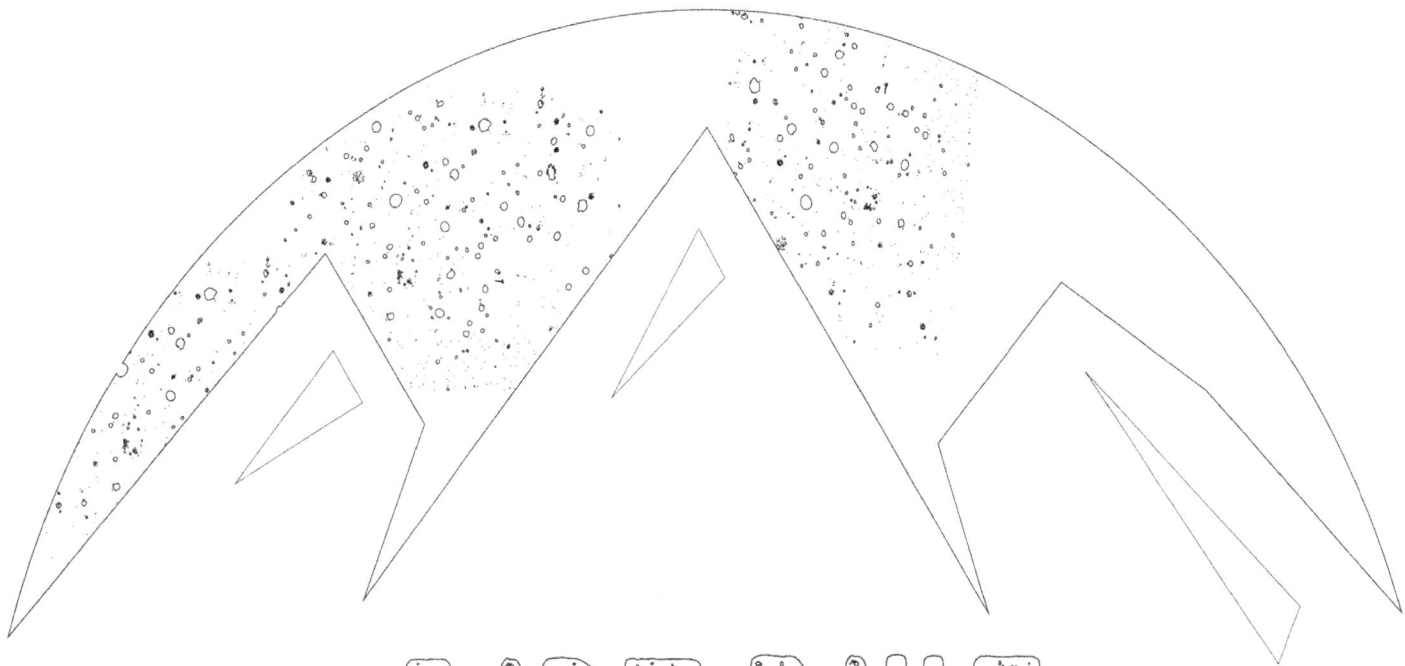

DIRT BIKE

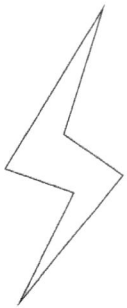
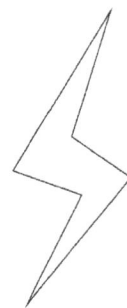

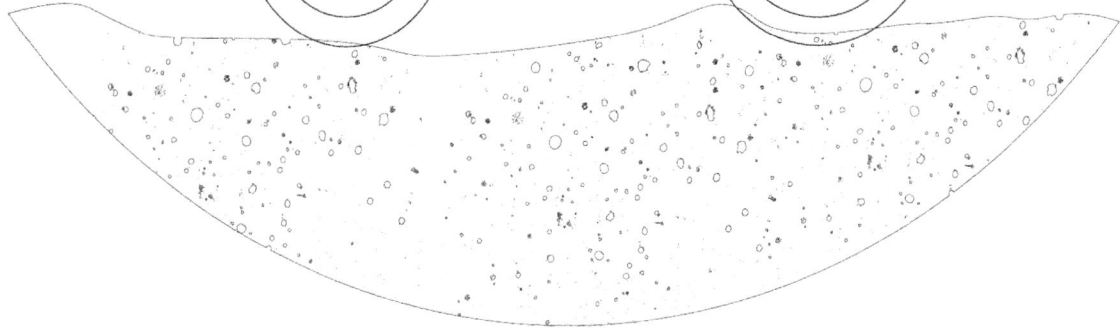

EST. XXI

WHY BE NORMAL?

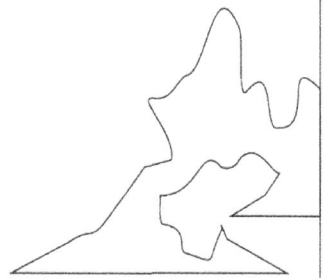

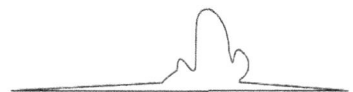

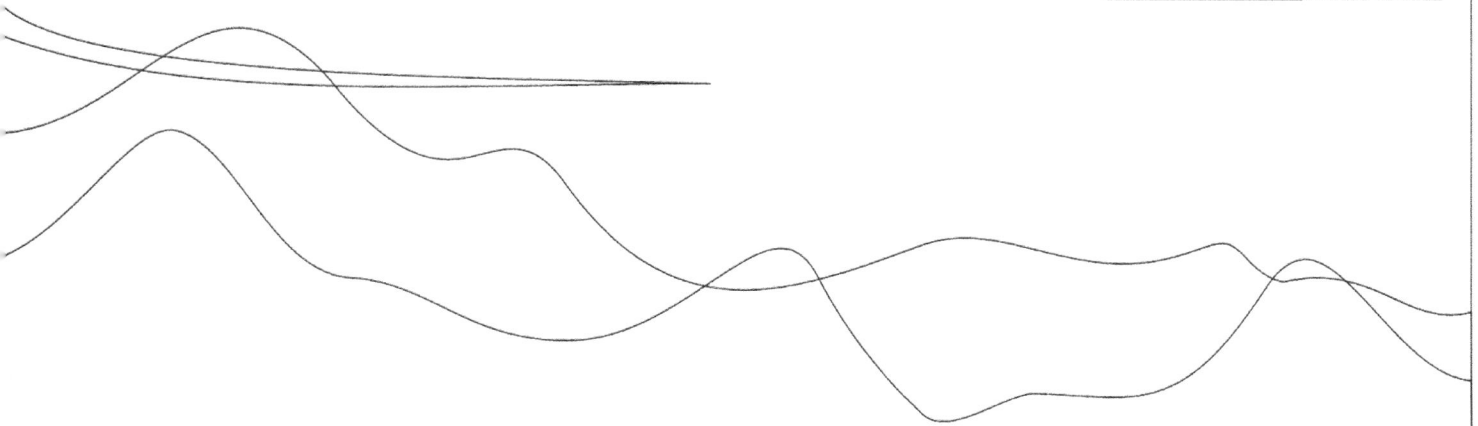

EST

1976

Live Fast Die Young

MOTORCROSS

CHAMPIONSHIP

The truth
IS OUT THERE

RARE!

MOTORCROSS

one

two

three

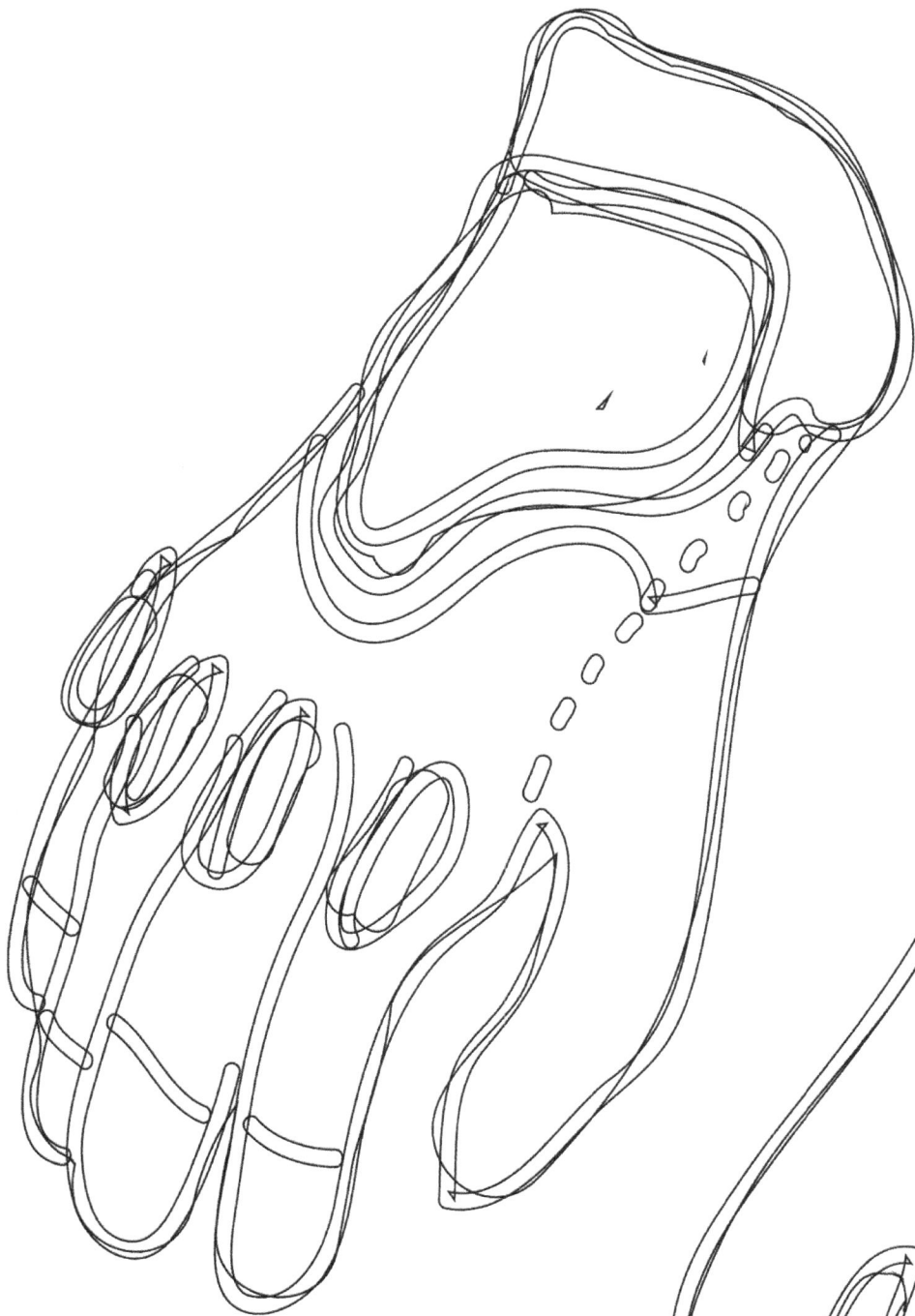

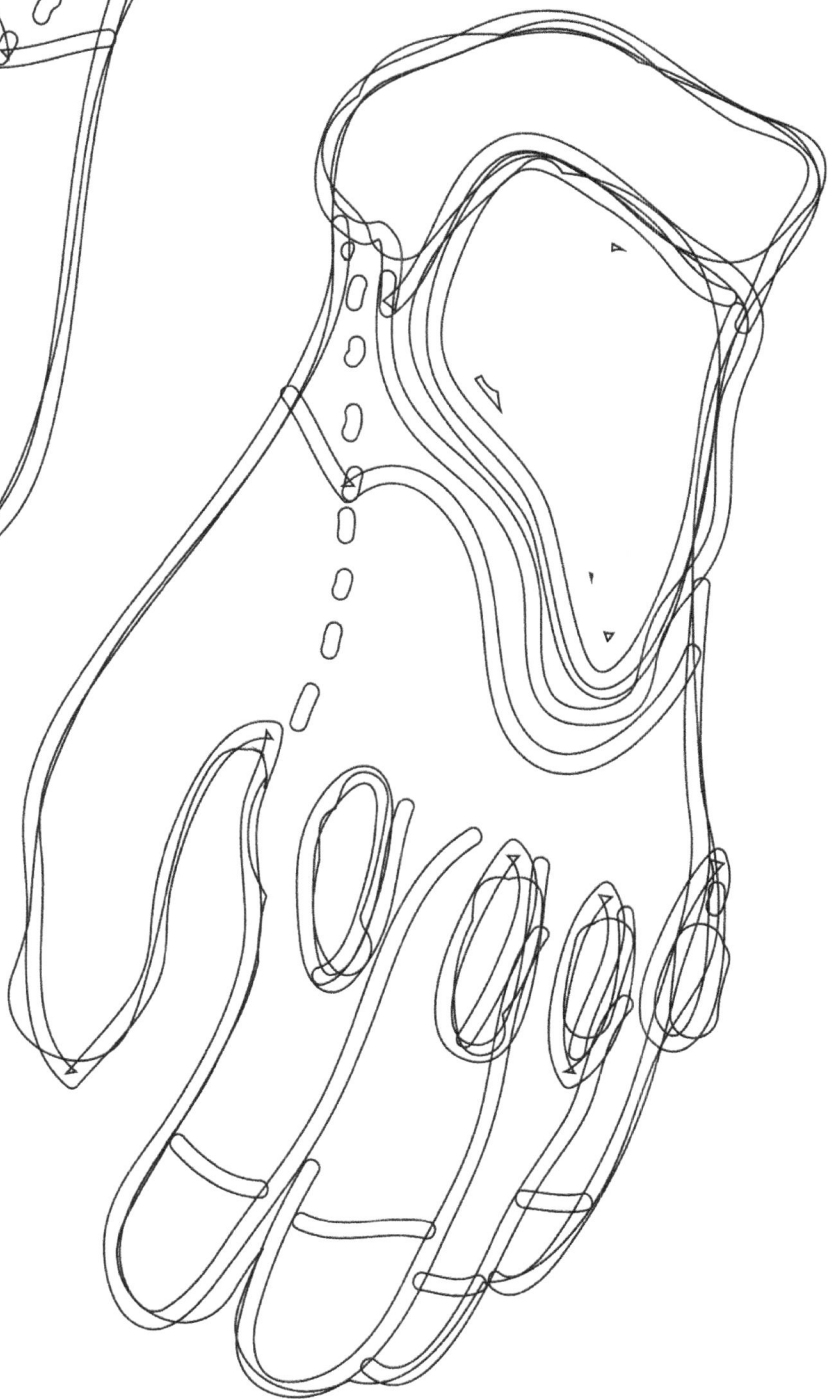

LOOK!!!

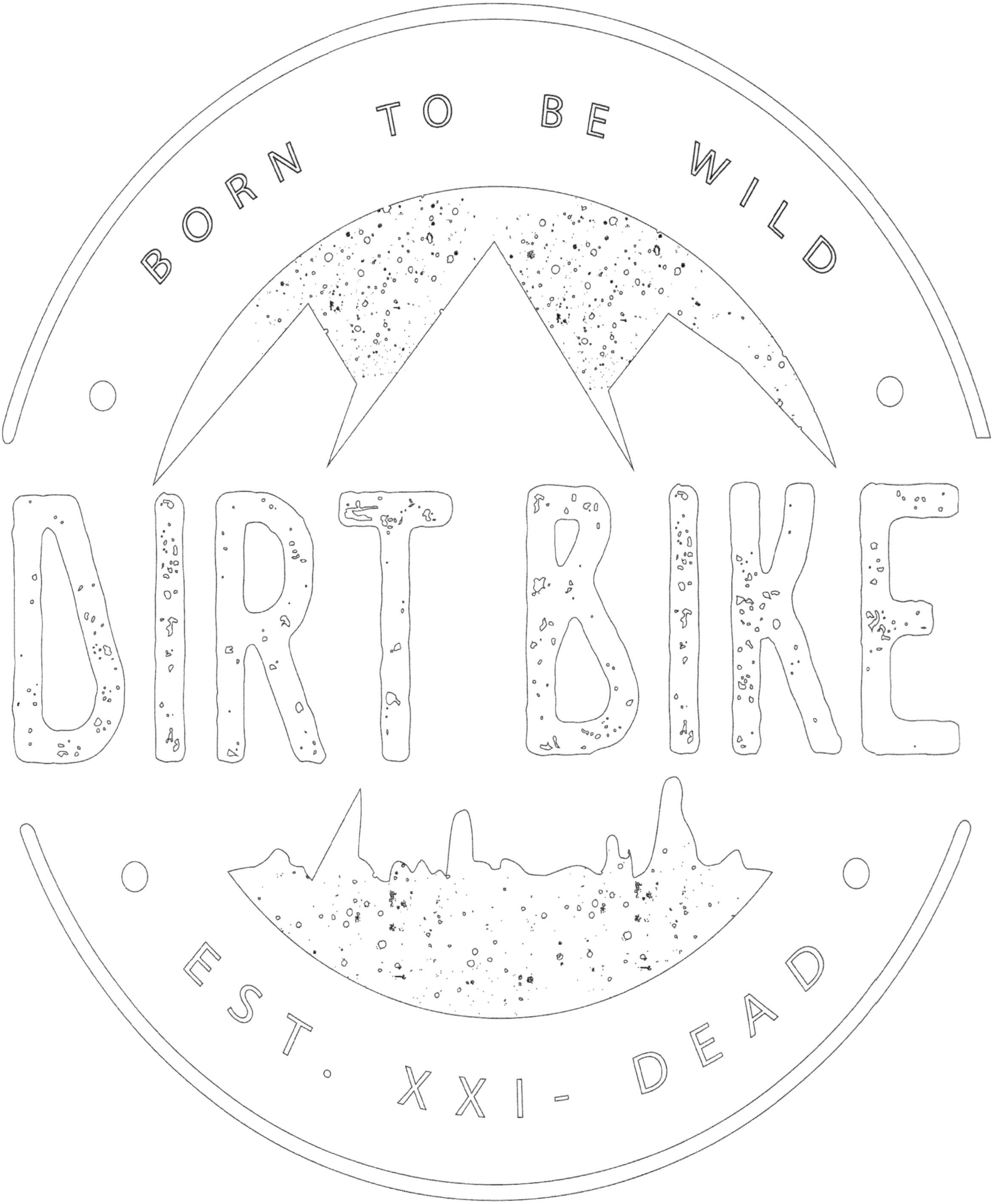
BORN TO BE WILD
DIRT BIKE
EST · XXI - DEAD

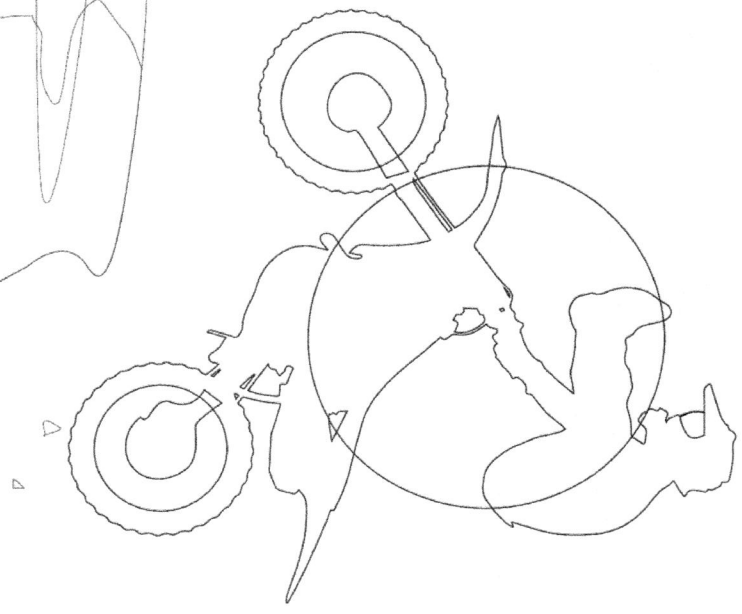

The Best VIEW Comes after the HARDEST CLIMB

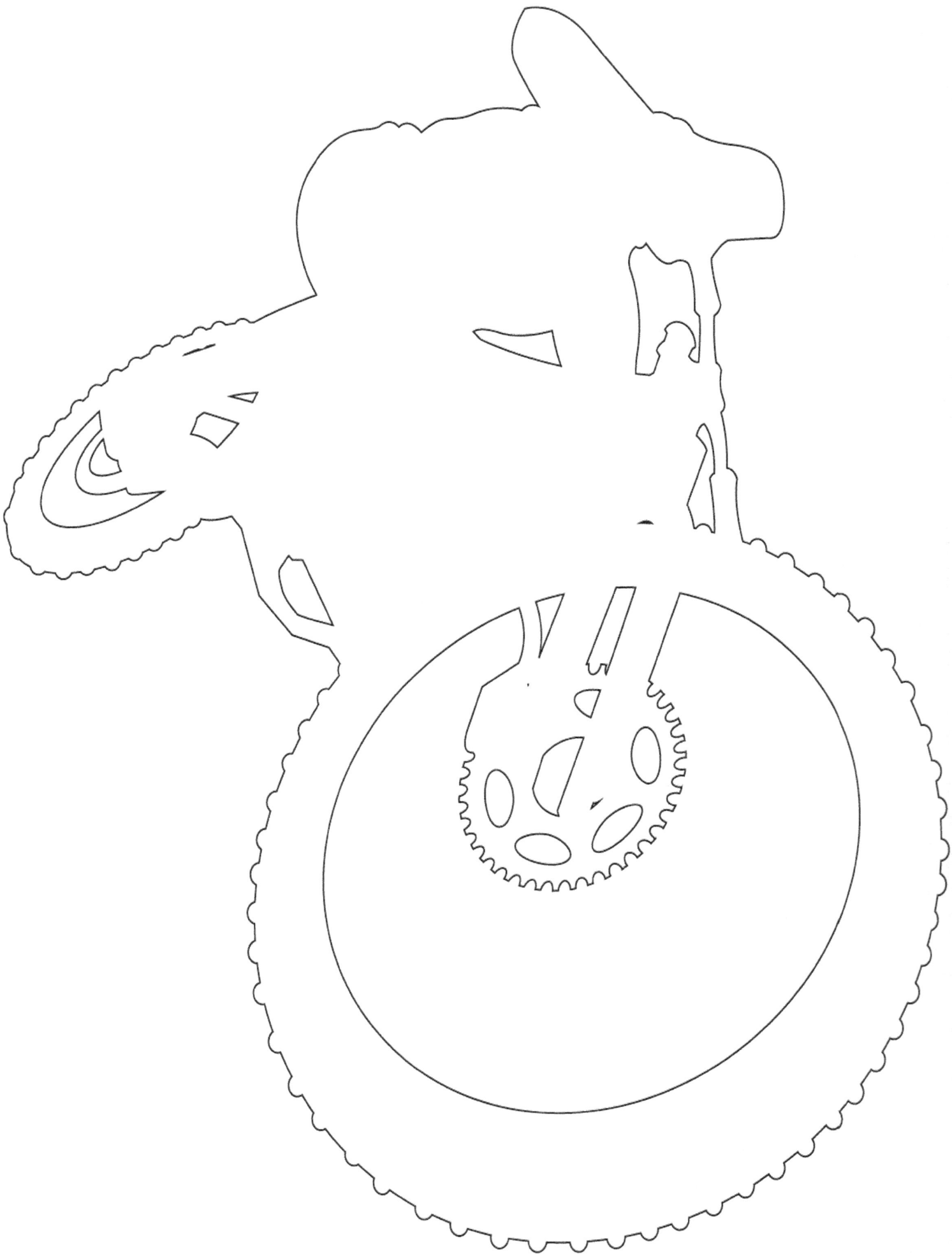

I LOVE YOU MOM

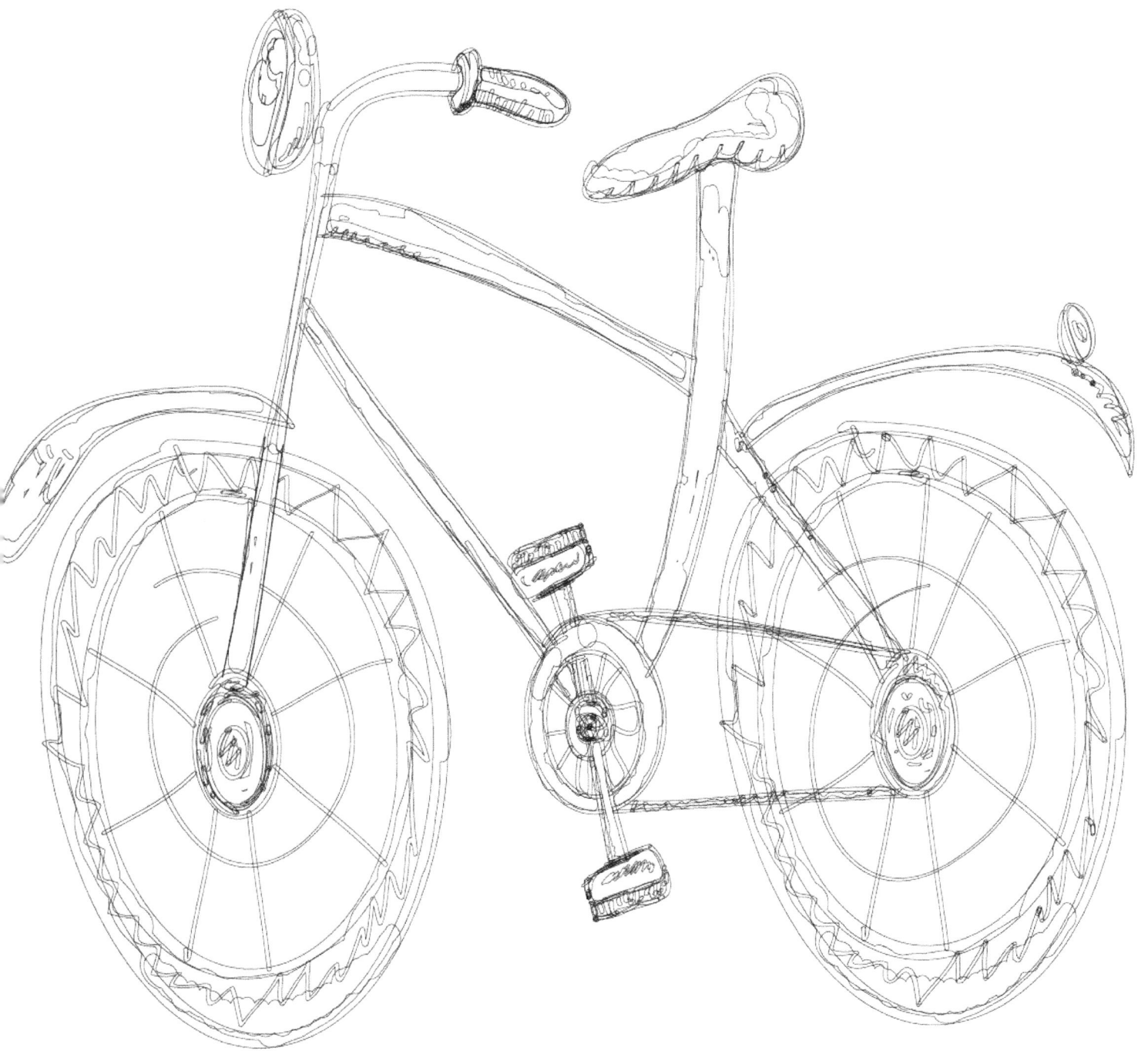

I ♥ MY BICYCIE

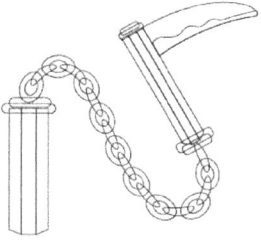

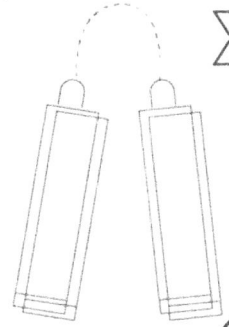

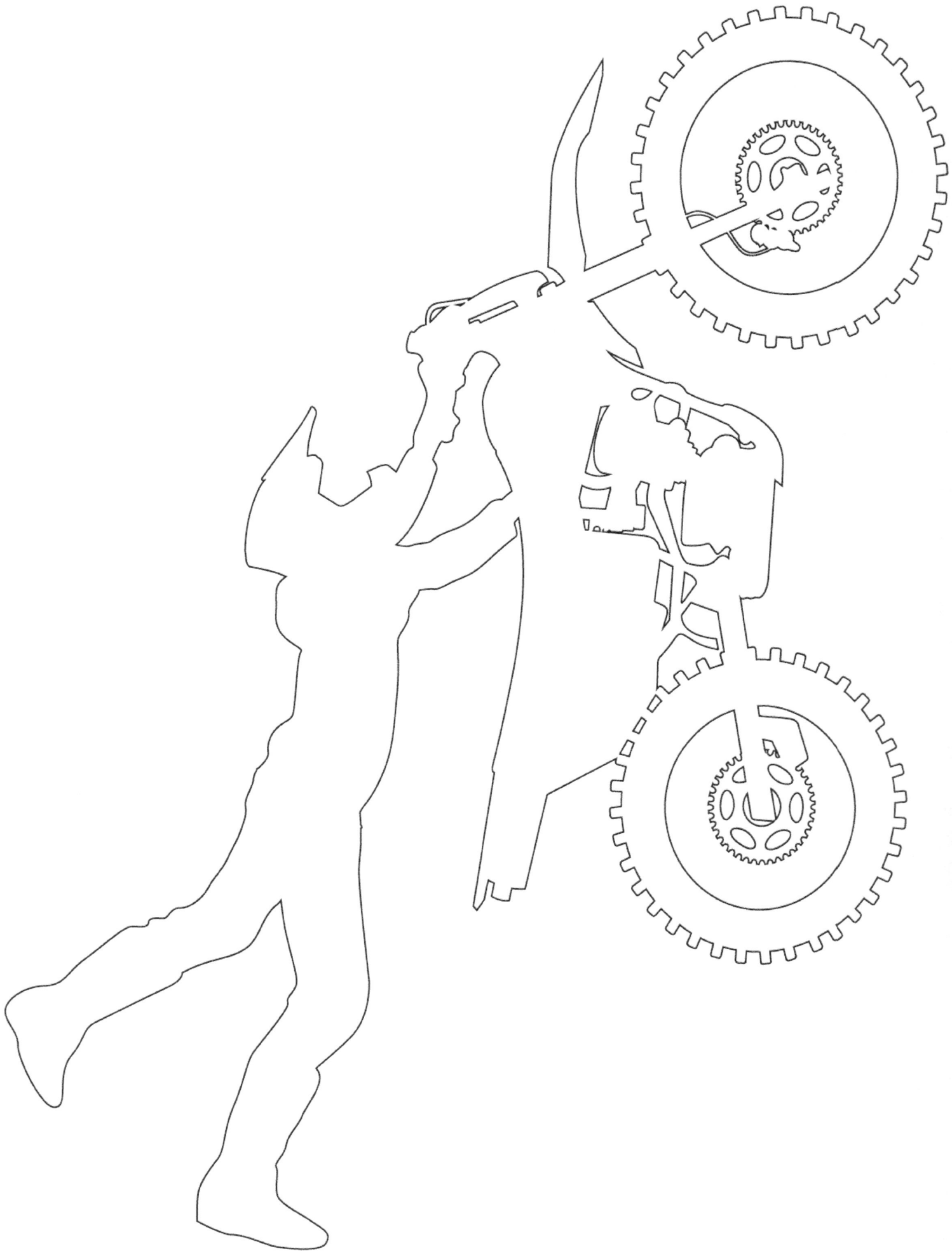

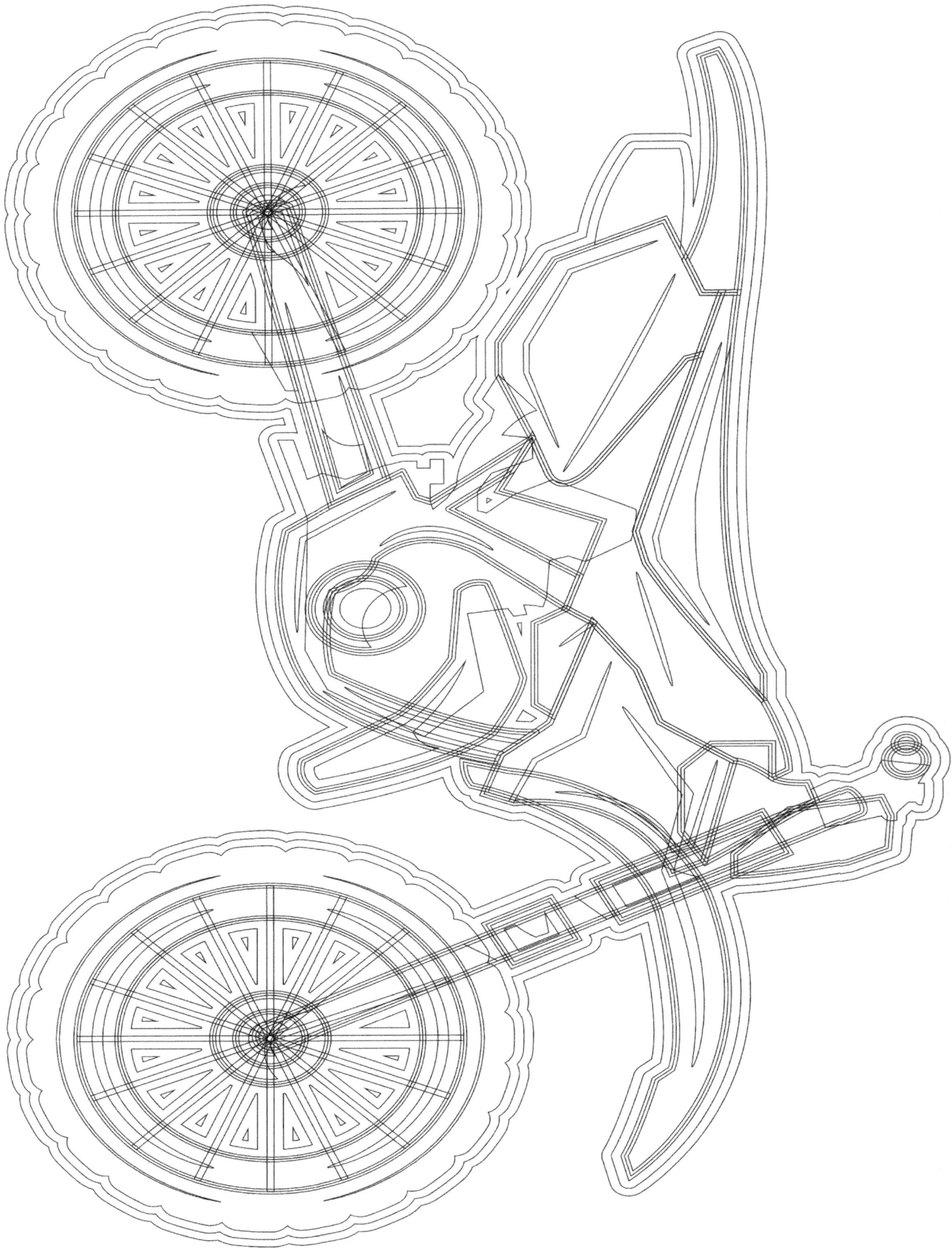

Okay

EXTREME SPORT

LET YOUR MIND WANDER

RIDE IT

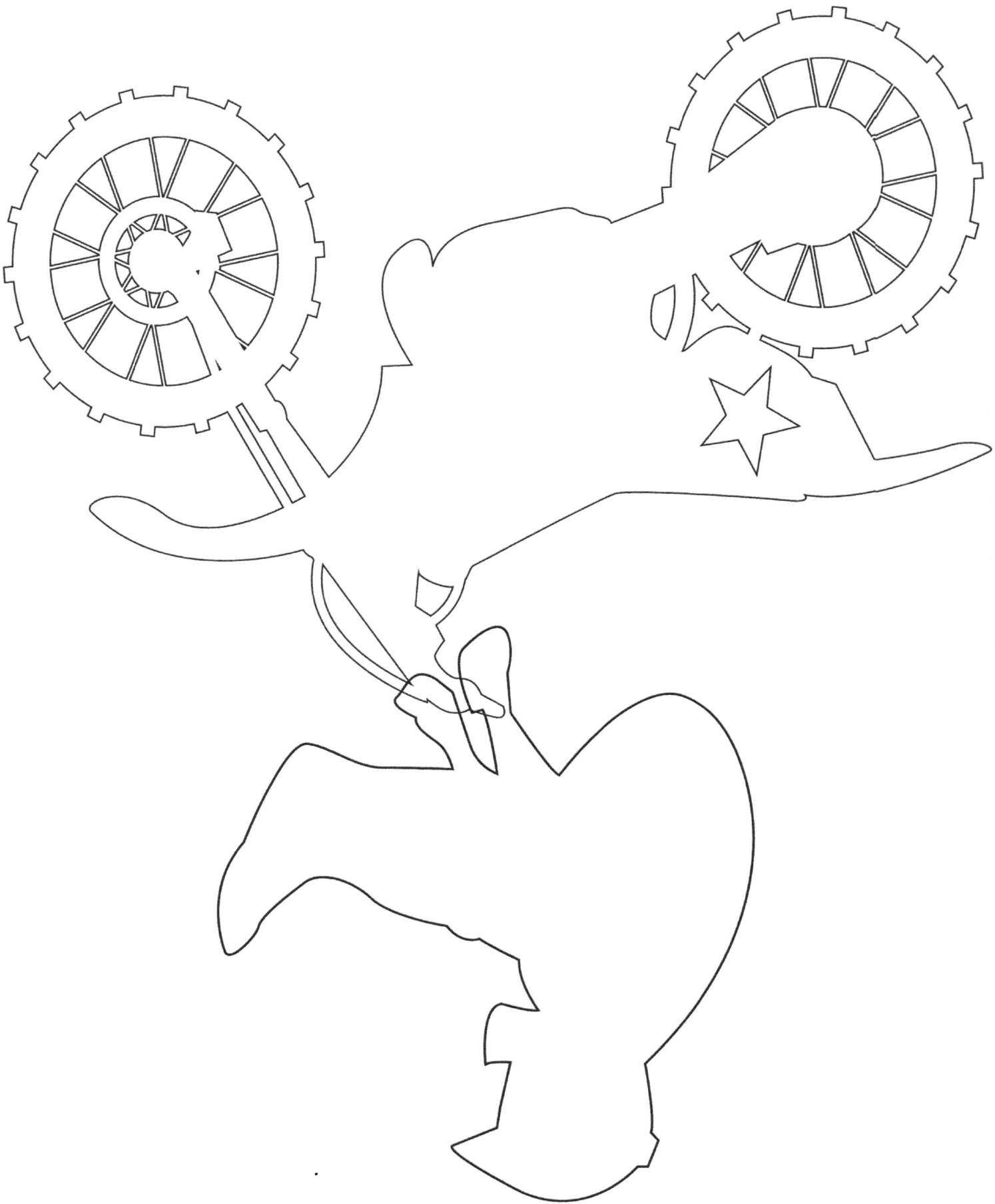

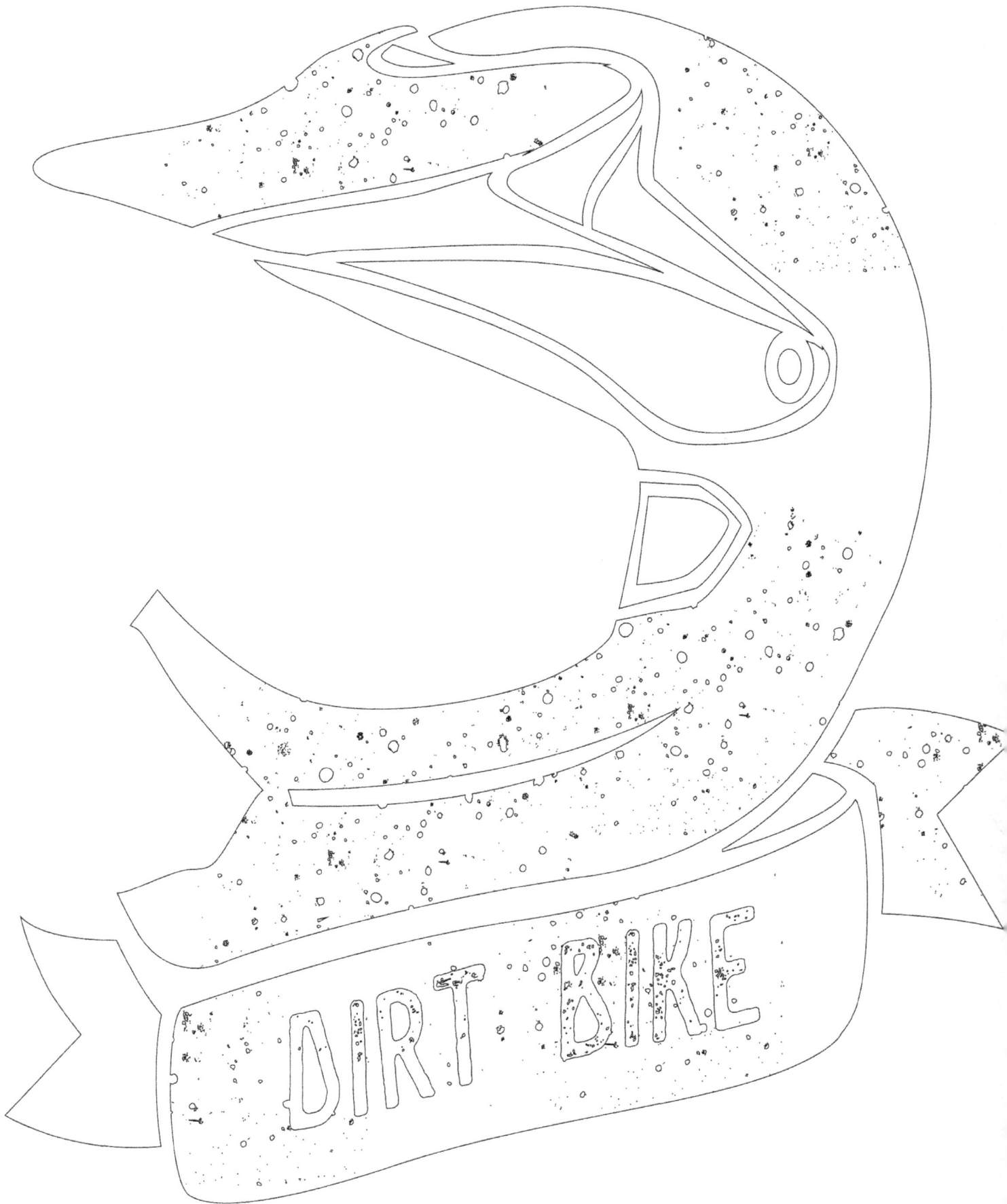

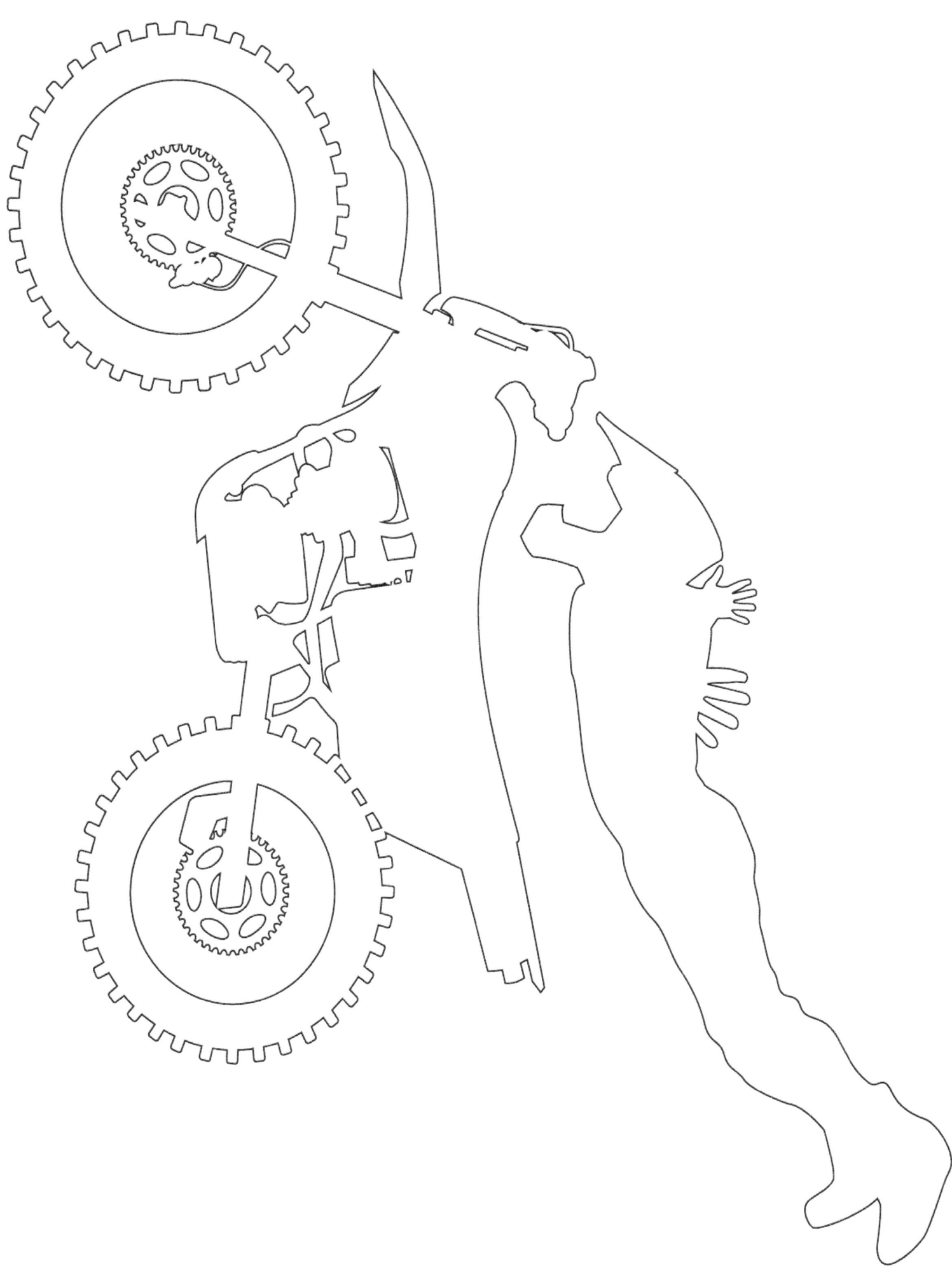

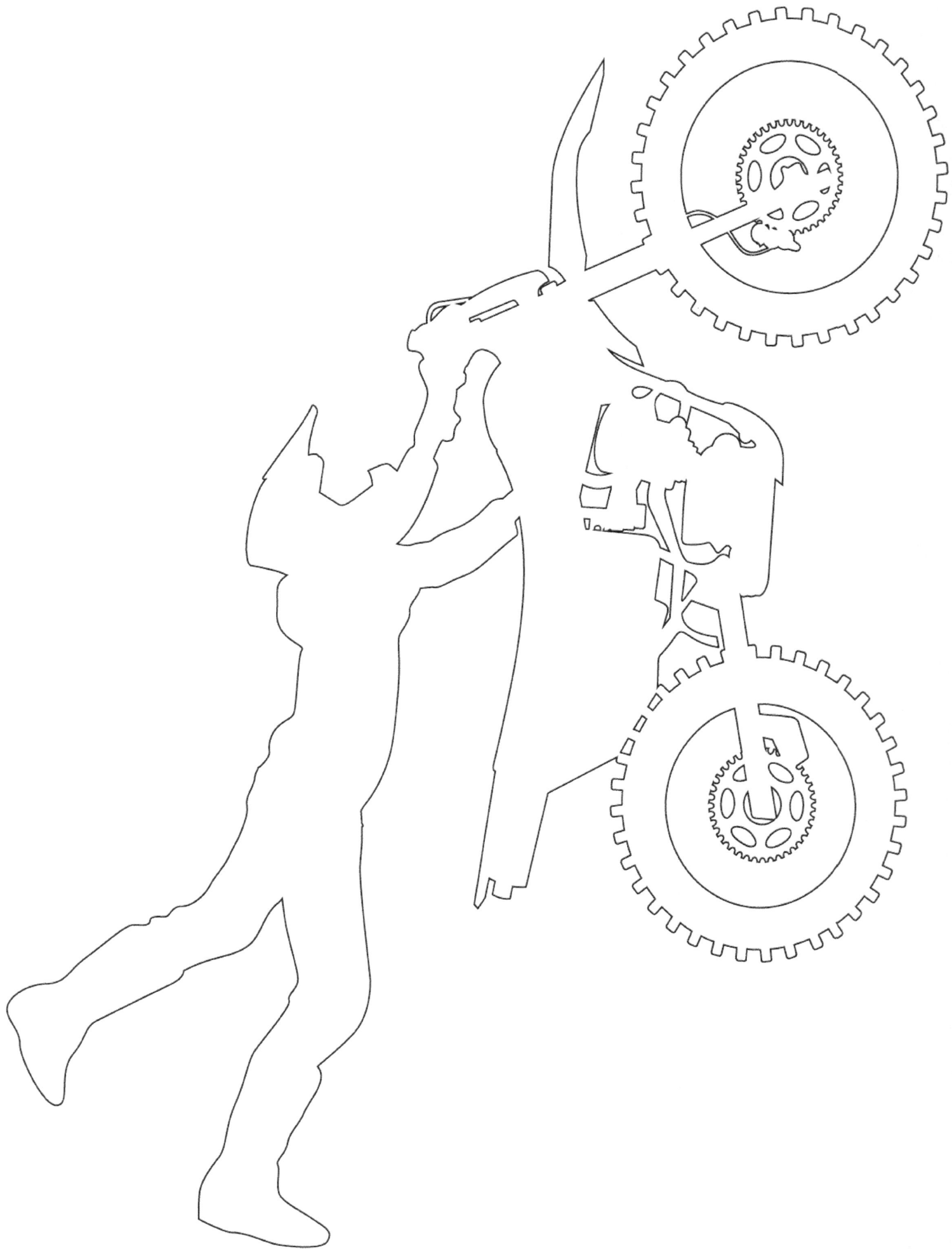

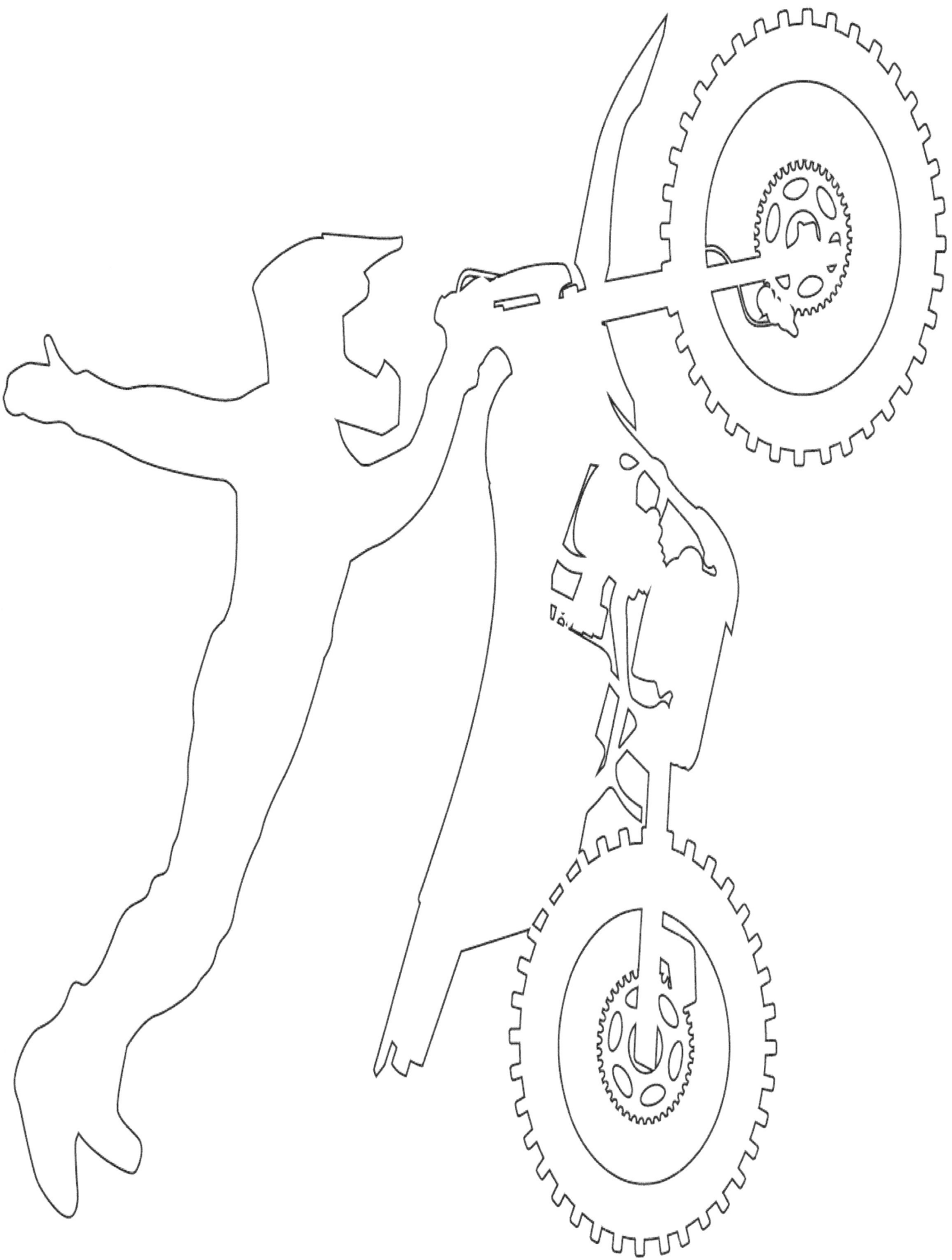

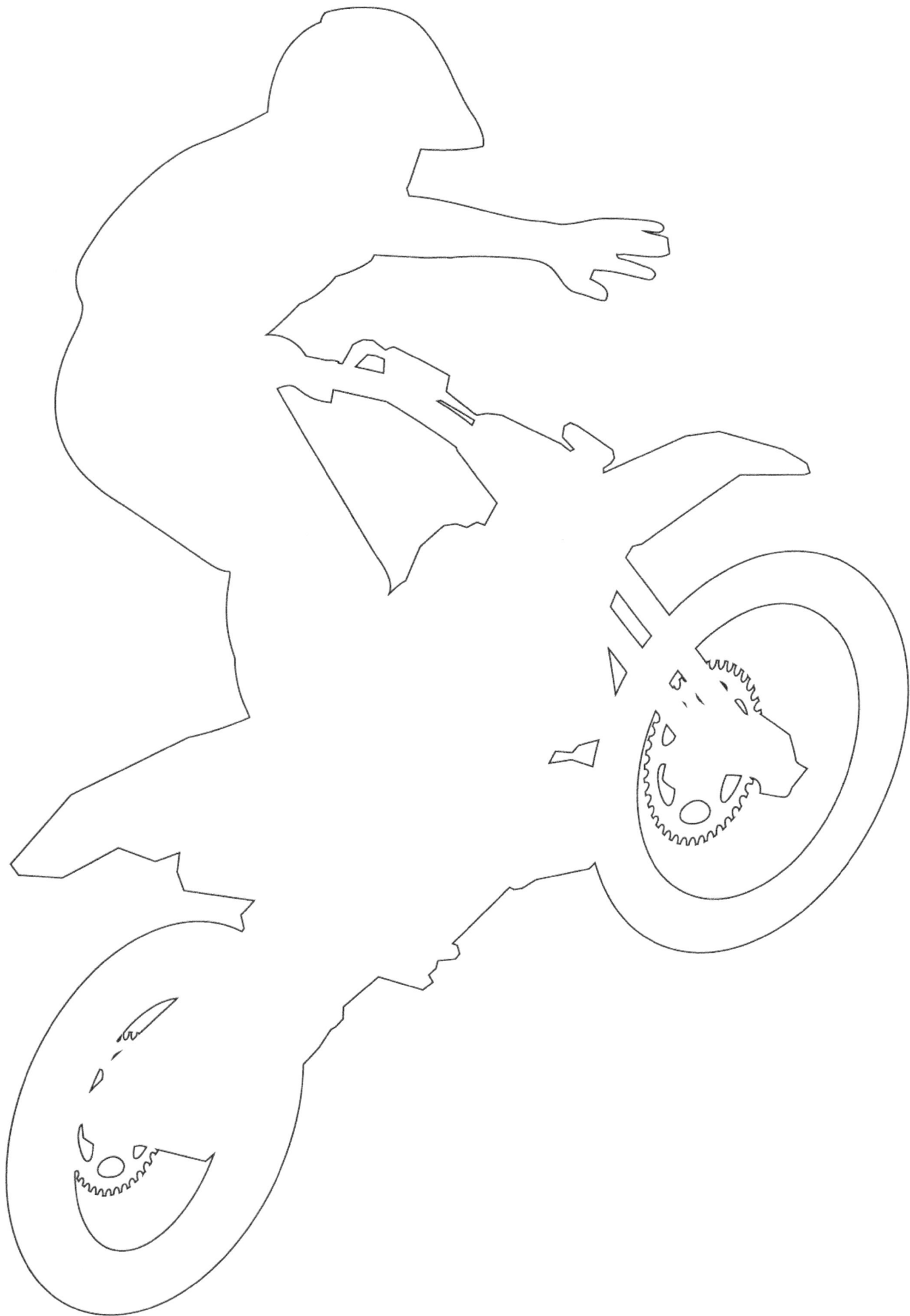

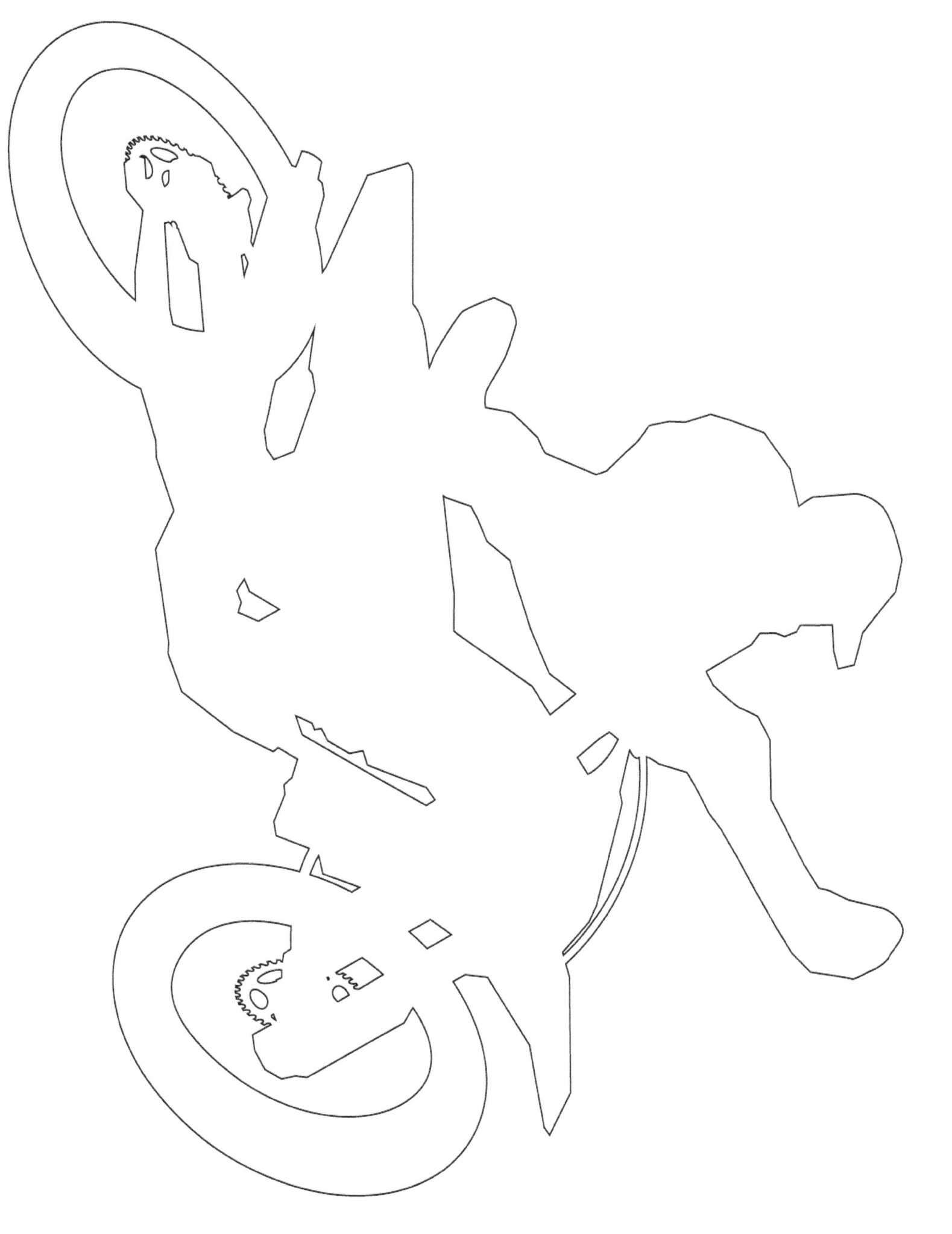

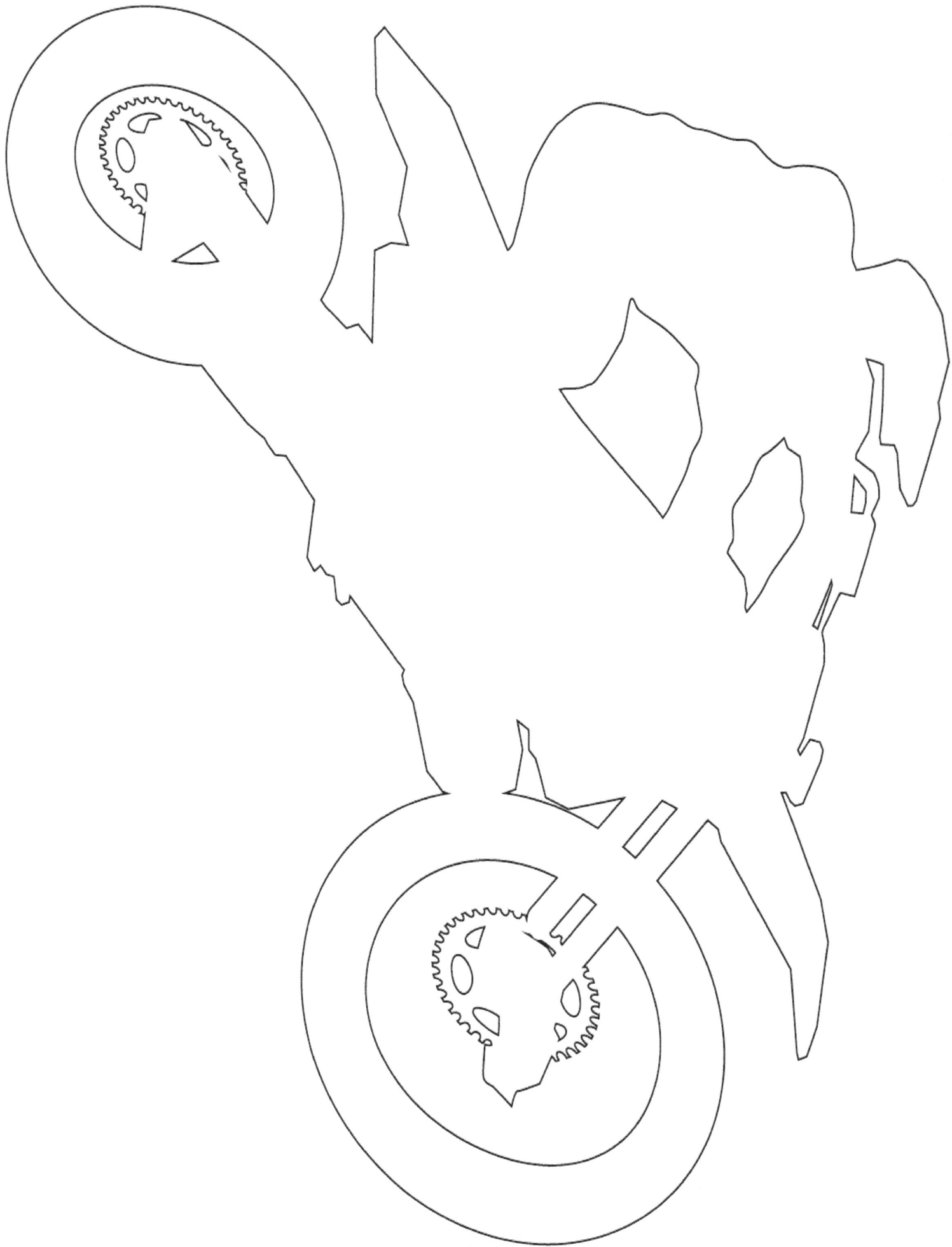

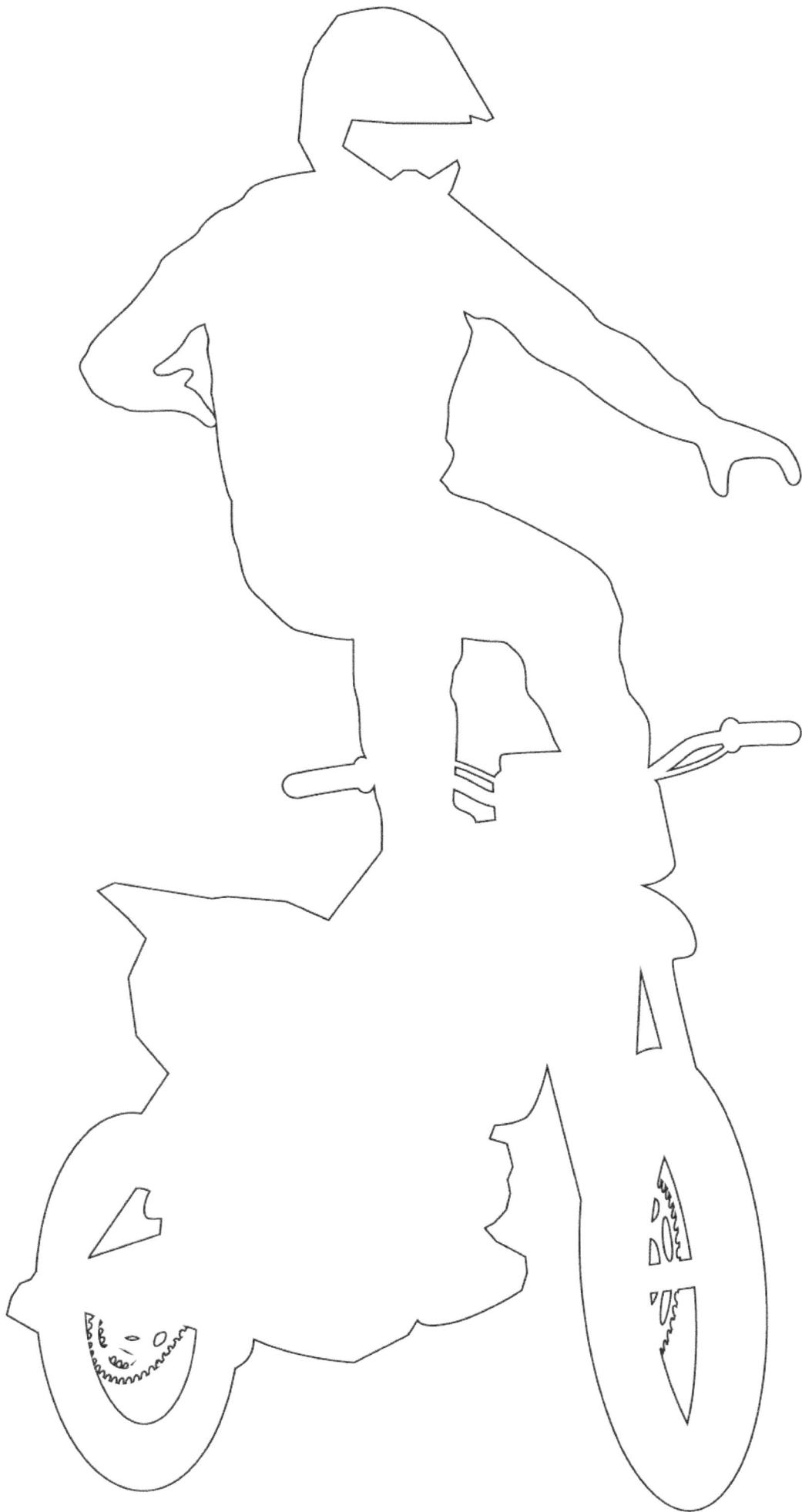

MOTORCROSS
CHAMPIONSHIP

Thankyou
You Are Awesome

Dear Magnificent Being

Producing this book was a **one-man operation**, and it took a **lot of hard work** to bring this quality content to you guys. I don't have a huge budget like other big publishers for advertising.

If you like this book , please spend a moment to add a review on amazon.com. This will help others to find the book. A Little Cute Video Review Goes A Long Way To Support Me.

Each and everyone of your reviews is paramount to me and for my survival as it helps me to compete against larger corporations.

I am **forever** grateful for your support .

Made in the USA
Monee, IL
27 September 2022